ETIQUETTE GEMS REVEALED

Charlotte Mweemba

CONTENTS

DEDICATION

This book is dedicated to Ben, for his immeasurable
love

ACKNOWLEDGMENTS

Profound gratitude to my faithful friends, Daniel, my life guru, Mable, Natalie, Ndita, Vichaya, Suzyo. Lushomo, Karen,and Chiku for their unwavering support. To my family, thank you.

To my beloved son, Chawanzi who I love and adore without measure for his patience and unwavering support, thank you.
Special thanks go to Thomas and Makisa for their steadfast support and for tirelessly making this publication possible.

INTRODUCTION

We often encounter one person or another that displays behaviour we consider inappropriate. Bad habits can be spotted from a distance. A badly bred grown man devoid of etiquette stands out in the crowd like a large rock among pebbles. The man wearing a pink and red chequered suit and blue tie at a restaurant speaking loudly on his phone for all to hear will stand out in the crowd compared to the one dressed in an ordinary suit that speaks only to the person on the other side of his phone. It's the conduct of an individual that determines how they will be perceived by others and that display how well-versed they are in the rules of etiquette.

Etiquette means being endowed with socially acceptable mannerisms. Although unwritten, the value and benefits of these rules are of great significance. People often underestimate the power of societal rules and the adverse impact that their non-compliance. Adherence to rules of etiquette, earns one respect, likability, and trust.

The idea of writing this book was inspired by real observations of people visibly lacking proper etiquette. I decided to study the subject further but came up empty in my quest for sources.

In writing this book, we took time to study basic principles of etiquette that have developed over time. Like change, the rules of etiquette have and continue to evolve with time, varying across cultures, age groups and people. An example of this is the advent of the infamous Covid 19, a pandemic which has irreversibly changed the standard manner of greeting, the handshake. The pandemic brought to the fore the extent of human interaction and exchange of fluids 'droplets' we never took notice of. This culminated in a dramatic change of behaviours that include social distancing and wearing of masks, things we never did before. This may mark the death of the traditional handshake as we know it, although the rollout of the vaccinations may mitigate it.

Regardless, there are certain common threads of etiquette that though informal, are so common that they have become generally accepted as universal and cut across several spheres including age, colour, religion, creed, tribe, and geography.

This book highlights the basic rules of contemporary etiquette.

CHAPTER 1
THE FIRST ENCOUNTER

'We don't know where our first impressions come from or precisely what they mean, so we don't always appreciate their fragility' — Malcom Gladwell

There is an unexplainable and mystic chemistry that goes on between two individuals during the first few seconds of their first encounter, as inevitably we form a mental image of the other person. We naturally form opinions about people during our first meeting, this is so regardless of the medium of communication, be it by phone, e-mail, or in-person. During a physical encounter, we would have formed an opinion about the other person, on sight, even before we hear their voice, just by merely looking at them be it on account of their facial expression, demeanour, physical appearance, dress, voice, race, language, gender or accent. As more time is spent interacting, our opinions about the other person are either validated or changed altogether.

Those first few seconds will usually make or break any prospects of creating or building any future relationships. In the words of Elliott Abrams, 'first impressions matter'. Experts say we size up new people in somewhere between 30 seconds and two minutes. Chewing gum, wearing a cap or earphones, reeking of alcohol during the first encounter will certainly not guarantee a second encounter. People's impressions of others will determine how they will relate to you, hence the need to be well-vested with the rules of etiquette.

In those first few seconds, several factors inexplicably and concurrently come to play:

The facial expression

> 'It is only at the first encounter that a face makes its full impression on us'— Arthur Schopenhauer

The facial expression worn by a person on the first encounter, can relay a message of warmth or coldness. An open facial expression augmented with a warm smile is more welcoming than a stern and cold look.

On the face are several other subtle factors that impact one's perception of another in a substantial way. A neatly shaven face, properly brushed teeth, a fresh fragrance, makeup, eyebrow shape, lip and hair colour, dress and jewellery type may all relay a positive image during the first encounter even before a single word is uttered.

Eye contact

Eyes are connectors. Making eye contact when interacting conveys openness, interest, sincerity and honesty. It is non-verbal communication yet very important and not only shows that one is genuinely interested in the other person but sends other positive signals.

The Smile

> 'A gentle word, a kind look, a good-natured smile work wonders and accomplish miracles'— William Hazlitt

One priceless attribute peculiar only to mankind is the ability to smile. Its strength is overlooked and often underestimated. It can light up even the darkest soul that encounters it, while brightening and energizing those that wear it. A smile helps build an excellent first impression and great energy. It exudes warmth, positive body language, openness and is in a subtle way an invitation for further interaction.

On the first encounter, the smile must be sincere and modest. A large ear-to-ear smile in a typical business set-up may relay the impression of overzealousness as opposed to warmth. The circumstances surrounding the first meeting subtly dictates what is appropriate. A modest smile on a first encounter transcends boundaries and its proficiencies are endless.

Body language and grace

We can judge and form opinions about other people just by looking at their faces and body language. Body language impacts other people's perceptions of us. The body speaks louder than the voice. It is important to depict positive body language in our interactions with others. Unacceptable behavioural tendencies such as looking up at the ceiling, folding arms across the chest, making faces, smacking lips, rolling eyes, fidgeting, scratching, crossing legs while standing are all examples of body movements that speak negatively to others. Poise and appropriate posture leave room for open and meaningful communication with third parties. In some cultures, it is considered intrusive to be physically too close when facing someone who is not an acquaintance, friend or family member.

Despite being intangible, it is also important to exude grace in our interactions with others. The word 'Grace' is derived from the Latin word, 'Gratus' which means pleasing and thankful. It's no wonder it is associated with meanings such as virtue and charm. Grace is a virtue that is necessary for our everyday interaction with fellow human beings.

The Greeting

The handshake

There are certain universally accepted ways of greeting. The handshake is the commonest. However, the advent of the infamous Covid-19, which triggered the universal prohibition of the handshake, replaced it with fist bumps, and left the future of the old handshake in limbo. The strong V-shaped emphatic handshake and most recently hugs have become a part of our culture.

Hugs are often reserved for family and people with a degree of familiarity between them. A handshake (or fist bump) in the business sense is arguably, still by far, the most acceptable way of greeting. You must show an interest in the other person by stretching out your hand, as these are indeed some of the innate ways of exuding good energy towards the other person.

Forbes[i], on its website aptly describes the handshake, albeit with reference to business.

> "A good handshake consists of a full and firm handclasp with palms embraced web to web. Shake up and down once or twice, coupled with a sincere smile and eye contact. Avoid the extremes of either a weak limp handshake or an aggressive bone-crushing one. Strike the right balance—firm enough to convey confidence yet matched to the strength of the other person. Treat men and women with equal respect when shaking hands. Gender makes no difference, and either one may initiate the handshake."

Basic rules of etiquette dictate that you do not cling to another person's hand for longer than is necessary, especially on your first encounter, irrespective of how appealing they may look. It is inappropriate for one to have to break out of your grip because of a long-winded handshake.

The Hug

A hug is ordinarily an embrace of two people which

involves the wrapping of arms around the other person's upper body, usually the chest or waist. Among intimate persons or close associates, be it family or friends, the hug may be followed by a kiss on the mouth or from cheek to cheek. Other cultures traditionally kiss the upper hand as a way of greeting, usually the men to the women. The menfolk, unless very familiar, will normally not embrace one another in the ordinary sense but rather rub their shoulder sculptures or pat hugs. Greetings by way of hugs are increasingly becoming a part of universal culture and are often a reflection and expression of the relationship between two people. This privilege should not however, be abused.

Regardless of the relationship, there are still rules of etiquette that govern hugs. Whether to hug or not depends on the prevailing circumstances. Hugs must be subtle and respectful, not clingy and squeezy. Lest they are considered intrusive and an invasion of privacy, which in some cultures might be construed as sexual harassment. Hugs must be reserved for those relationships that have earned themselves that right. It is inappropriate to hug someone on a first encounter unless the environment or circumstances permit it.

At the most, a hug must be a gentle embrace touching only the upper side of the other person's back in the process and not lowering the hand to the extent of impropriety. Whatever the case, it is always necessary to remember to maintain those unwritten boundaries.

The introduction

An introduction to another provides an opportunity to

know the other person. Applicable rules of etiquette will depend on the culture, age, profession and social standing of the person introducing themselves or being introduced. Regardless, ensure that warmth and grace are exhibited from the outset. That is what makes people memorable.

A person can either introduce themselves or be introduced to a third party by another. During self-introduction, etiquette implores that you take the approach of introducing an opening statement that will create common ground with the person you intend to introduce yourself to and then proceed to introduce yourself. For instance, 'that was a great Speech Sir. I am Sharon Johnson, editor of the Sun Newspaper. Pleased to meet you.'. In other instances, you may be more forthright as in, 'Good morning. I am Sharon Johnson from…, which would be followed by a smile or offer of a handshake. The circumstances will dictate which approach is appropriate.

An introduction of others, whether formal or informal, can start by, 'Mr. Son, please meet Miss Johnson. Miss Johnson, meet Mr. Son". Then the usual, 'Pleased to meet you', protocol sets in. It is also advisable to repeat the name of the person to who you have just been introduced, as in, 'Pleased to meet you, Carol!'. In any event, it is argued that repeating a person's name after being introduced to them will help you remember it and save you the embarrassment During introductions mention the name of the person you are more familiar with first.

What is prudent through it all, is to exude warmth and positive body language.

In most parts of the world, formal business relationships require the use of formal titles. Mr., Mrs.,

Miss or Ma'am unless and until the other person gives you the authority to be addressed by their first name. For instance, at a formal meeting, 'Good morning, Mrs. Kay?' Mrs. Kay may respond, 'I prefer to be called Susan. May I call you James?'. First name basis in any set up does not happen as a matter of course. The bottom line is you need to earn the right to address one by their first name.

Once the introductions are made, we move on to the conversation.

> 'We sometimes encounter people, even perfect strangers, who begin to interest us at first sight, somehow suddenly, all at once, before a word has been spoken'-Fyodor Dostoevsky

---

[i] https://www.forbes.com/pictures/ejjl45kdmm/a-confident-handshake/#11f1884073c9,

CHAPTER 2
THE CONVERSATION

'Wise men speak because they have something to say; Fools because they have to say something'—Plato

Words

Words are tools through which discussion is had. Words, therefore, are the primary constituents of discussion. Everything else that follows, including tone and pitch, facial expressions and general body language, all but accentuate or otherwise give meaning to the spoken words.

Words have power

In the words of Suzy Kassem, 'We cannot control the way people interpret our ideas or thoughts, but we can control the words and tones we choose to convey them. Peace is built on understanding and wars are built on misunderstandings. Never underestimate the power of a single word and never recklessly throw around words. One wrong word can change the meaning of an entire sentence and even start a war. And one right word, or one kind word, can grant you the heavens and open doors.'

Words are potentially double edged-they possess the power to build and conversely, to destroy. Due to the enormity of the power possessed of words, caution must be exercised in their use. Societies have revolted after moving speeches. Great men and women alike have throughout the ages changed the world by words. Martin Luther King Junior's' famous 'I have a dream' speech delivered in 1963 addressed to over 250,000 people is said to have set the tone for change during the American Civil Rights Movement in the 1960s and is believed to have had a profound influence in the emancipation of civil rights in the United States of America.

The Golden Words

Politeness is reflected in the words we speak. Adherence to the rules of etiquette falls in that bracket. It makes us likeable, easier to interact with and get along with other people, even strangers, enabling us to create meaningful relationships with others. There are Golden Words, certain universally used and accepted words that when used are soothing and can warm even the sternest of hearts and often create a platform for further engagement. 'May', 'Please" Thank you' 'I am Sorry', 'Excuse me', 'I forgive you', all have the power to change any situation. The use of these words relays the message that the speaker is polite, respectful and well-bred. It is these virtues that render these words priceless.

There are basic rules of etiquette that govern conversation. These rules are general, not cast in concrete and depend on the prevailing circumstances like the degree of familiarity between people.

The Conversation

Conversation is a dialogue between people. It is a two-way process between the speaker and the recipient. The initiator of the conversation speaks, and the recipient listens and should listen attentively, responsively and courteously to the other person and vice-versa. Showing interest in the conversation of another or others enhances interaction and paves the way for further interaction leading to future relationships, the seed from which networks are born.

The NO-NOE'S

There are six general no-noes for conversation. Never for any reason discuss, SEX, RELIGION, POLITICS, FINANCES, WEIGHT and now SEXUAL ORIENTATION with people you are unfamiliar or just acquainted with. The discussion of these subjects can only take place between people whose existing relationships permit.

The DO'S

There are generally acceptable rules of etiquette that apply to most situations. These are:

- Pay attention and show interest when the other person is speaking.
- Always give others an opportunity to express themselves. Let the converser finish their side of the story. Never remove another's story from their mouth let alone finish it for them.
- Avoid interrupting the other person's conversation, lest they lose their line of thought. You may politely interrupt if you need clarity on an issue. Even when one is talking to another, it is prudent to wait until they end their conversation and if you really must interrupt, politely excuse yourself.
- Never correct another in the presence of others. Doing so is discourteous, unless done with tact and respect and only if necessary. One such situation is where the person conversing does not have the full and accurate facts relating to a particular subject and could be misleading to the listeners. It may be justifiable to respectfully correct them and provide an accurate picture with the basis for the source of that information, or alternatively, it can be done in private, although the inaccurate information would have already been disseminated.

For example:

Mr. A - 'Apparently the building at the corner is co-owned by Mr. J and his daughter X which they intend to convert into a mixed-use estate.'

Mr. B- 'Sorry to interrupt, I happen to be one of the Consulting Engineers engaged in the upcoming project, the building actually belongs to the Municipality and is slated for the construction of a modern hospital.'

- Be respectful of other people's time and avoid taking more time than allocated by the other person during meetings.
- Restrict the conversation to the issues between the persons present. Eavesdropping and adding to conversation at the next table with other people exhibits ill-breeding and a blatant lack of manners.
- Listen more than you speak.
- Avoid criticizing or blaming others.
- Avoid engaging in arguments.
- Admit it when you are wrong and apologize. Hard as it may sometimes be, saying sorry only takes a fraction of a second and has never hurt or changed anyone. People have more respect for people who take full responsibility for their wrongdoing than those that do not.
- Avoid giving excuses.
- Avoid overindulging in discussions about yourself and your personal issues especially to people you just met. Rather find a subject that may be of interest to the other person. Bragging falls in this category. There's nothing that closes doors for future interaction like being exposed to someone who blows their trumpet to the point of overlooking everyone else. There are many financially emancipated people who prefer to keep issues of their wealth private.
- Don't overindulge in discussions about your personal issues especially with people you just met. You might be unfairly judged and risk losing

the opportunity to reveal your real self, blocking prospects of any future interaction. Always keep your personal life private. Remember people only know what we tell them.

- Do not complain about personal issues like relationships, money, and work. There will always be a time, place and appropriate person to vent to. There is nothing as exhausting as being around chronic complainers and whiners.

- Do not engage in personal attacks on any third party especially in their absence.

- Do not smoke in the company of others, if you must, politely excuse yourself.

- Avoid excessive drinking especially around people you are not acquainted with. It is prudent to keep the quantity of alcohol being consumed moderately. Alcohol is notorious for its ability to trigger the discard of all manner of etiquette, leaving you feeling guilty the next morning.

- Avoid making, answering calls or chatting on phone applications that require you to type during conversations. It is not only distracting but also undermines constructive conversation and shows outright disrespect for the other person. If you must take a call, please politely excuse yourself and walk outside to take the call privately.

- In formal meetings, activate the 'silent' mode function on your phone. Phones and their ringing tones have the tendency to interrupt normal human face-to-face interaction and can be destructive to family and other relationships, if not managed properly.

- Whispering loudly or speaking at the top of your

voice.

- No matter how hilarious, do not guffaw or laugh out loud but do laugh moderately.

- Avoid gossip let alone speak ill of others, regardless of how seemingly 'juicy' the story. You have no idea who is in the audience and their relationship to the person under discussion. People, their networks and the extent of their respective relationships are not written on their foreheads. Remember the adage, walls have ears. To the sensitive person, client or guest, that is enough to put off any potential future interaction no matter how promising. No one wants to be around energy drainers, that's what ill-talk does- it drains energy. A friend holding a relatively high office once passed a nasty comment about a subordinate co-worker to a fellow co-worker. Two days later, they met at an event and lo and behold, she discovered that the two co-workers were in fact married to brothers and had a great relationship.

- Avoid conversations that may refer to events or situations which may result in any level of emotional stress, pain or discomfort to those around. A few years ago, shortly after the Rwanda genocide, on a trip with a delegation from various African countries, someone made an insensitive remark about the genocide in the presence of a Rwandese national, triggering an emotional response from everyone, instantly changing the vibe from happy to sombre. In such situations, it is prudent to immediately apologize, change the subject or just stay quiet. The rule of thumb is to be sensitive to the present audience when engaging in conversation especially when little is known about the audience.

- Avoid conversations in subjects you know very little or nothing about lest they cause you embarrassment.

- Do not be judgmental or force your opinion on others. Instead, endeavour to respect other people's beliefs and opinions.

- If you must disagree, respectfully do so, e.g. 'I respectfully beg to differ with your opinion because ......' is more courteous than a blatant, 'that is a blatant lie...'

- Do not repeat any unpleasant story about another unless it is necessary. The unspoken rule is never to repeat anything to anyone that you learn about if it may cause trouble, distress or pain to others. It's okay to let some things pass.

- Never ridicule the age, fashion sense or personal imperfections and inadequacies of others regardless of form.

- Never discuss any potentially discriminatory attributes such as nationality, race, tribe, religion, handicap, culture or beliefs of others.

- Respect other people's privacy. People will only tell you what they want you to know. It is inappropriate to break personal boundaries by prying into other people's business if it is none of yours. The rule of thumb is to stick to your lane.

- In relation to the above, never inquire about the intricate or personal details of another's illness-it is none of your business. I remember visiting a relative at the hospital when his co-worker arrived in the room and immediately picked up the file with the Doctors notes at the foot of the bed and started flipping through it. It had to take the patient himself, to politely request that his privacy be respected, prompting the co-worker to return the file where he had found it.

- Etiquette dictates courteous adaptability to different people, circumstances and situations. We encounter different people every day. Being able to interact with various people at all levels and respectfully adapt to their level, while being sensitive to their feelings and treating them with the respect and humanity they deserve. Remember, there is no limit to the people we can learn from.

- At the end of every conversation, remember to say thank you and respectfully bid your farewell.

'Those who decide to use leisure as a means of mental development, who love good music, good books, good pictures, good plays, good company, good conversation-What are they?

They are the happiest people in the world.'- William Lyon Phelps

CHAPTER 3
THE DRESS

'You can have anything you want in life if you dress for it'— Edith Head

Dress is a broad concept. Dress not only refers to clothing but extends to a whole lot of other aspects like jewellery, makeup, handbags, hair and fragrances that we wear, which all come together to form 'dress'. The dress starts from the head and down to the feet, all of which play a role in determining how we are perceived by others.

Dressing and public perception

Clothes are subject to individual taste. The appropriateness of dress depends on factors like the event, venue, crowd and time. We are quick to form perceptions of others merely by looking at their dress, even before they open their mouths.

A woman clad in an ankle-reaching dress with flat shoes may give the impression of being conservative. The one in a dress slightly below the knees with high heels will likely give the impression of being a modest professional while the one in a dress slightly or way above the knee may be indicative of being liberal, with the latter perhaps, too liberal.

What is deemed appropriate varies from place to place. Like everywhere else in the world, what is appropriate dress is subjective. There are however certain generally acceptable standards of dress etiquette that should be adhered to.

Fashion and apparel

Regardless of how modest you are, it is important to endeavour to keep up even at the barest minimum, with reasonable prevailing fashion trends. The fashion industry has and continues to evolve. What was trendy a few years ago is no longer trendy and sometimes, dressing up in 'old-fashioned' attire will make you stand out in the crowd as odd.

Fashion is a matter of individual taste and preference. Some people are inclined to never miss a fashion trend while others will let some of these trends pass. Very few ordinary people will wear most of the clothes worn by top models on the runway in their day-to-day lives, let alone on special occasions.

It is always prudent to dress appropriately and for comfort while retaining and reflecting your character. A selection of the appropriate colour, cut, length and shape of attire should be borne in mind. Further, the event and audience should also be a factor in the choice of dress. For instance, a bright red dress worn above the knee at a funeral would be completely inappropriate. The point is that you should avoid looking out of place or creating a wrong impression of yourself. Dress speaks volumes.

Jewellery and accessories

Jewellery and accessories also form part of the dress. They comprise the decorative personal embellishments like necklaces, bracelets and rings. They are worn to complement and enhance a person's overall look or dress. We will collectively refer to jewellery and accessories as 'jewellery'.

Like all manner of dress, rules of etiquette should be observed in the wearing of jewellery for both men and women.

Jewellery etiquette

The rule of thumb with jewellery is to be modest, while maintaining the overall look. The type of jewellery worn depends on one's personality and the nature of the event. While there are no standard set rules, there are certain basic guidelines:

- For the neck, one set of jewellery is sufficient. A layered and balanced combo may work for a celebratory event
- For the fingers, avoid excessive and over-sized pieces of jewellery unless the piece is a bold one that accentuates the overall look. For the ordinary person, two sizeable rings per hand is suitable. If the ring is large, it is not appropriate to wear more than one ring on that hand.
- Do not wear distracting and noisy jewellery.

- Ensure that the bracelets, earrings, necklace have harmonized colours and metals. Harmony in this case is not about uniform colours but refers to a combination of colours that blend with the outfit.
- For earrings, it is recommended to choose those that blend with your face shape. For example, dangle and teardrop type of earrings will be suitable for a round face, as they have the effect of elongating the face. Hooped or rounded earrings on a round face will exaggerate the circular shape of the face. The same applies to sunglasses.
- Studs and small loops are appropriate in the workplace or at conservative events.
- When hair is worn up, more of the face and neck are exposed making a short necklace appropriate as it draws attention to the neckline.
- For long hair worn down, curly or bulky hair, more dramatic earrings can be worn.

Fragrances

'There are some smells that kind of stop people in their tracks and make them turn around and run the other way. There are scents that will stop them in their tracks and make them come closer to you-that's the power of scent'.... Fragrance evokes so much. So, scent is very, very powerful.' — Bryce Faulker, New York-based Fragrance Expert (quoted by Hannah Vincent-Style Salute)

Fragrances form part of a person's dressing and can be

regarded as a kind of accessory. Fragrances are often loosely collectively called perfumes regardless of composition. The 'smell' reverberating from a new acquaintance goes a long way in creating that first impression.

Fragrances come in various types based on their respective overall scents-citrus, floral, fruity, oriental, spicy, woody or green. Like clothes, fragrances are a matter of personal preference. It is important to know and understand the different varieties of fragrances and how they are created. Etiquette steps in to highlight which fragrances are appropriate for which event.

Types of fragrances

Fragrances that are ultimately bottled for our own personal use are assigned different names, (the difference lies primarily in the concentration of the essential oils they are made from) which in turn determines the price of the fragrance. The higher the concentration, the higher the price. The concentration will determine how long it lasts and when it is appropriate to use it.

Fragrances are branded and packaged for both men and women, some of them being unisex. Highlighted below are the various types of fragrances and their oil concentrations[ii]

- Eau Fraiche- Alcohol and water and lasts for up to an hour when worn.
- Eau de Cologne usually refers to male scents and lasts up to two hours when worn.
- Eau de Toilette a light spray which lasts up to about four hours suitable for day wear.

- Eau de Parfum-Contains 15-25% pure perfume essence and will last for about 5-8 hours, suitable for everyday wear.
- Perfume-The most expensive and concentrated of all fragrances, with 20-30% pure perfume essence and when worn, can last up to 24 hours.

It is said that our body chemistry determines the fragrance's effect including the aroma, with individual bodies interacting differently with certain fragrances. A fragrance sprayed on a testing card and that on the skin may be different.

Wearing fragrances and their descriptions

Various terms are used to describe scents. Terms like floral, cool, fresh, heavy, light, musky, mild, bubbly, delicate, gentle, pungent, exotic, tangy, sweet, pleasant, warm, strong, exquisite are all visual descriptive words for fragrance scents.

Fragrances influence the people we interact with and do create impressions. The first date with a person reeking of a fragrance with the semblance of an insecticide is guaranteed no second date. The same applies for overpowering fragrances. There are times we have been greeted by the smell of a fragrance even before the wearer of the fragrance appears.

Like clothes, fragrances must be worn appropriately. It is obviously not advisable to wear a very strong fragrance at a funeral. A clean and subtle fragrance might suffice especially considering the sombreness of the event.

According to Hannah Vicente of Style Salute who provides guidance on wearing fragrances, on a day event, like work, date or other similar gatherings, a neutral and floral fragrance will suffice. In the evening it is unisex, rich and exotic fragrances may be appropriate while for family events, soft and fresh fragrances may take the day.

While this may appear as a complex guide, it's easier to keep it fresh and clean. It is also permissible to fuse different fragrances provided the fusion doesn't become offensive.

[ii] source-www.sonoriam.com

CHAPTER 4
OFFICE

'People will typically be more enthusiastic where they feel a sense of belonging and see themselves as part of a community than they will in a workplace in which each person is left to his own devices'— Alfie Kohn

The office is where we often spend most of our productive and attentive hours of the day. Ordinarily, the workplace has people from various backgrounds, holding different positions and stratified by an organizational structure which creates a hierarchy of positions ranking from the highest office to the lowest.

Inevitably, the office requires interaction with other individuals within the organization. Whatever the case, every individual employee plays an integral role in the successful running of the organization. Human relations are core and predictably therefore, etiquette.

Organizational dynamics are broad and diverse and

can have far-reaching consequences on organizational performance. Like the first meeting, the non-verbal cues of dress, make-up, walk, demeanour, tone, attitude, all interact in the workplace and form the basis upon which an employee will be perceived by others. We all carry a part of our pasts, positive and negative. There might be that one special co-worker who is so bitter and wants everyone else around to feel their pain. Regardless, a conscious and deliberate effort should be made to make our lives and those around us in the workplace, a joy or at a minimum, bearable. Never be the reason a co-worker despises their place of work.

Etiquette should therefore step in to define acceptable behavioural patterns even in the workplace for each member of staff personally and in their interaction with co-workers, clients and visitors.

Superiors

Superiors have a profound influence on their subordinates in the workplace. Regardless of character and personality, superiors should exude an ambience of not only confidence and authority but also grace and integrity. They must comply with the established organizational rules. Treating staff with respect and fairness, always sets the pace and tone for an organization tied with chords of cohesion. An organization that works as a team is limitless in its potential.

Self-respect and respect for subordinates

As goes the adage, respect is earned. Superiors should respect their staff when addressing them which includes words spoken, tone and body language. A superior should also exude self-respect in the workplace. A superior that is vulgar and constantly comes to work wreaking of alcohol and unkempt hair will soon lose the respect of everyone in the organization. The superiors good reputation is critical.

The reprimand

The reprimand of the erring subordinate should be conducted in line with proper established channels, with respect and without demeaning the dignity of the subordinate, regardless of their wrongdoing. Reprimands must ordinarily be done in private.

Some superiors get apparent gratification from yelling at subordinates in front of clients or their co-workers. Yelling at a subordinate in public is not a show of manliness or authority but is in fact a dent on the superior's own integrity, in the eyes of the subordinate and the audience. It is a display of utter lack of respect for others, including the audience around.

Boundaries

While it is important to engage in occasional social conversations and get to know basic personal information about their staff where necessary, superiors must do so within certain defined boundaries. Over-familiarity in the workplace can destroy work relationships. Personal life should, be kept personal.

Family should also be kept within a reasonable distance, if not completely tucked away from the workplace by all means, except for perhaps typical family-owned businesses. A retired male colleague tells a story of having worked in an organization for over 35 years and his wife never having gone beyond the entrance of his workplace. While it may not always be harmful, over-interaction between family members and co-workers has the potential to breed chaos.

While some have ended up happily ever after, romantic relationships or associations with the opposite sex, male or female and particularly between a superior and subordinate should be avoided. A female subordinate romantically involved with her superior may perceive themselves as having 'acquired' unfettered rights around the workplace and this may negatively affect her relationship with her co-workers. The superior, male or female, might also be unable to give proper instructions and reprimand the subordinate with whom they have an improper relationship in the workplace. Superiors must themselves exude self-respect in their conduct and interaction with others within the workplace. In addition, relationships around the workout might give rise to issues surrounding sexual harassment in the workplace, posing serious reputational and criminal hazards for both the individuals concerned and the organization.

Conflict

Conflict among superiors must be managed to the exclusion and where possible, without the knowledge of junior staff. As a rule, never gossip or speak ill about your co-superior with a junior. Civility, respect, courtesy, openness and sincerity with co-workers are key to dispute resolution. Raised voices, inappropriate language to a co-worker are attributes of not only ill-breeding but exhibit a blatant deficiency of the rules of etiquette.

Equals

Like everyone else, those that rank equal within the organization's hierarchy must treat one another with mutual respect. You cannot therefore summon or order an equal to your office for official business unless of course it's a social call, which will also depend on the relationship between the equals. An equal should only be called where the circumstances require so, such as inviting them for a meeting in which their input would be required.

Dealing with Superiors

Superiors should be treated with all the necessary respect. The organizational policy will normally dictate how co-workers address each other, first name basis or more formally as in the use of prefixes such as Mr., Mrs., Ms., Sir and Madam.

Superiors from their conduct will determine how their subordinates relate to them. People have diverse personalities, warm-natured, serious and egotistical and several others. It is those with out-of-the-ordinary traits that often earn themselves nicknames in the workplace behind their backs.

The subordinates' behavioural expectations of their superiors are high, and the superiors must therefore conduct themselves as such. Superiors set the tone for the organizational culture.

Disagreement and criticism

Conflict is the inevitable consequence of human interaction. Superiors may be senior, but like all human beings can also be prone to error. The general rule is that they should regardless, be accorded the necessary respect. It is permissible to disagree with one's superior or another co-worker, but such disagreement must be done with respect, courtesy and politeness. 'Excuse me Sir, I respectfully beg to disagree...' is a respectful way of expressing one's disagreement. Differences must not be confrontational, arrogant, demeaning or antagonizing but must be civil and open. Caution should be given to the people around in doing so. It is advisable to raise divergent views in private. If it is trivial, not damaging or prejudicial let it pass. What is acceptable entirely depends on the circumstances.

A subordinate must avoid expressing controversial or otherwise prejudicial contrary opinions in the presence of visitors or clients unless it is necessary. This rule applies to equals and co-workers. The rule of thumb is never to degrade, belittle or under-estimate or deliberately out-shine your co-worker in front of others, especially those outside the organization. Likewise, the superior, in disagreeing or criticizing the junior, must do so both courteously and respectfully.

Sometimes a superior may disagree with a subordinate irrespective of the correctness and logic of the subordinate's point of view. The subordinate's views might even be the best option for the workplace at that time. Being open-minded and able to gracefully accept and embrace mistakes and errors, misjudgement or even rejection is a virtue that must be cultivated and exercised. As a subordinate, the truth will always be that once the superior has been advised, one's advisory duty to the superior is discharged. The decision lies in the boss' hands. It is not in the subordinate's place to force his views down the superior's throat in a take-it-or-leave-it approach, as this might even be construed as insubordination. Gracefully accept that he is the boss and that your views have been rejected and move on.

Even when the consequences of not heeding the junior's advice eventually unfold, the junior must still accept it and not bad mouth or ridicule the superior regardless of the magnitude of the apparent consequences. Where there may be critical consequences, it is advisable for the subordinate to put his views, opinion or recommendation in writing to the superior, sent through an email or other traceable platform addressed to the superior, for future reference. Some superiors have the tendency of blaming their subordinates when things go wrong and forget the advice they were given yet opted to ignore it. If necessary, a respectful reminder of how the events in the issue unfolded can be made, provided it is constructive and intended to enhance the interests of the organization.

CHAPTER 5
COMMUNICATION

'The most important thing in communication is hearing what isn't said'— Peter Drucker

Phone calls, e-mail, letters and social media

Communication lies at the core of humanity. Communication exists in verbal and non-verbal forms. The old saying, 'nothing lasts like a first impression' is as true in face-to-face contacts as it is on other platforms like the phone, e-mails, letters and social media. Communication is not just about spoken words, it is about all the other unspoken, unwritten and sometimes even inexplicable cues that can be felt or read irrespective of the form of communication. It is because of the absence of physical presence that rules of etiquette should therefore govern every communication on these platforms.

Phone calls

Phone calls may be formal or informal. Unlike personal interaction and its attendant cues, the phone requires communication only by voice. Therefore, the construction of words, the tone and pitch, all come together to relay the message being communicated. Cues such as warmth, anger, arrogance, happiness, hostility can all be read from a mere phone call. Sometimes, we even visualize the appearance of the other person through the voice.

Businesses, especially the service industry understand the value of the most important person in the organization-Front Office. That one phone call is often the first impression of a person or organization and may set the tone for prospects for future relationships.

Clear, distinct, and reasonably low tones should always be used during phone conversations, especially with socially unfamiliar persons.

Making the phone call

Safety first

Unlike the case in the past, technology has made the phone multifunctional. It keeps us in touch with family, friends, business associates and the entire world through its various platforms. The phone has become our mobile banks, our shopping centres, offices, entertainers and a whole lot of other things.

Phones have become an integral part of our lives and have in the process acquired immense power. Many of us cannot function without them. That said, the phone must still be used responsibly. Before making or answering a call, ensure that your own personal physical well-being is secured. Years ago, a friend made the decision to take a call while crossing a very busy road. He got distracted by the call and failed to check for on-coming traffic. The last thing the caller heard was a big bang followed by silence. The caller was safely seated at his office desk when he decided to make that call, which was intended to merely check up on the person who had at that moment lost his life.

Self-destructive habits such as messaging, speaking while holding a handheld device in the process of driving or in the middle of an assignment inevitably reduce one's concentration levels making one vulnerable to errors and accidents. Safety should always come first.

To make or take the call?

The effect of a phone call is that when the caller phones another, they are essentially demanding, at their own instance, that the receiver of the call stops whatever they are doing at that very moment and answer their call, whether they like it or not. That is the power of the phone caller.

The person called, in turn, has the power to decide whether to take that call or not. If it's not convenient or you do not desire to speak to that caller or it's not safe to do so-DO NOT answer. The lesson here is that not every call must be taken. It is your own phone, not the caller's phone, and you get to decide which phone calls to take and not the other way round. That is the power we possess but often neglect to use.

Etiquette dictates that the caller asks the other

person at the inception of the call whether it is a good time to talk. If not, the caller may request to be called back or ask what time might be convenient for the call. Modern phones are now fitted with automated Short Message Service (SMS) options such as, 'Can't talk now'. All those are intended to, among others, promote good etiquette and safeguard our interests. Let us therefore make use of them.

Focus

They say it takes about twenty minutes to truly focus on a particular task. Once distracted by a phone call or any other occurrence, you will require another twenty minutes to refocus which might carry on, all day.

Blake Thorne, in an article, *How distraction at work can take up more time than you think*, states, 'That's how many minutes of concentration you're losing. It takes an average of about 25 minutes (23 minutes and 15 seconds, to be exact) to return to the original task after an interruption, according to Gloria Mark, who studies digital distraction at the University of California, Irvine. Multiple studies confirm this. Distractions don't just eat up time during the distraction, they derail your mental progress for up to a half-hour afterwards (that's assuming another distraction doesn't show up in that half hour).'

It is important to manage phone calls and the time spent on them to ensure the constructive use of our time.

Phones can interfere with the building and sustenance of relationships including family. Time reserved for meetings, formal or informal, should therefore not be interrupted by unnecessary phone calls.

Overall etiquette dictates that phone calls should be made or taken when it is appropriate having regard to the necessity, audience, your location and safety. These rules also apply to texting and the use of mobile applications that require the user to speak, read or type.

The basic rules of phone etiquette

While we are at liberty to use our phones as we desire, there are certain practices that go against the rules of etiquette. Putting any of these behaviours into practice will immediately change people's perception of you and question your social standing.

Therefore,

- Never start a conversation with the other person before confirming whether it is convenient for them to talk.

- When you are aware that the person being called may not have your contact in their phone or you are not known to them, politely introduce yourself and highlight the subject matter of the call at the outset.

- Do not raise your voice or use offensive and vulgar language.

- Never hang up but rather politely wind up the conversation irrespective of the circumstances.

- Where the caller is unknown, politely ask the identity of the caller for instance, 'Sorry, may I know who this is?', rather than a blatant, 'Who is this?'.

- Never give out other people's numbers without their permission.

- When you have dialled a wrong number, politely apologize.

- Avoid dropping calls when interrupted rather politely ask if it's okay to call back or use the automated Short Messaging Service (SMS) function on the phone. It is recommended that you place the phone on silent mode to avoid getting interrupted.

- Avoid talking to someone else while on the phone with another.

- Do not continuously speak on the phone while in the company of others.

- Do not chew while speaking on the phone.

- Avoid putting any caller on the loudspeaker without informing them in advance or seeking their permission especially in the presence of a third party. What is spoken is usually only intended for the recipient and not for the consumption of others. There is often an echo in the background and the other person may be able to determine that they are on loudspeaker which may border around infringement of privacy and breach of trust.

- Avoid continuously remaining on a call where the 'call waiting' function is activated, rather call back later. While the call waiting function may be important to alert the phone owner of an impending call, there is a reason your call is not being taken, while on another call.

- If you must take a call, while on another call, following the 'call waiting' notification, it is acceptable to excuse yourself from the call to take the incoming call.

- Always switch off or activate the silent mode option on the phone before a meeting or any public gathering.
- Do not place a loud and disturbing ringtone on your phone. Keep your ringtone pleasant and simple. Avoid using songs as ringtones. While choice of ring tone is a matter of personal choice, remember, other people get to hear them too and may affect how others perceive you.
- Avoid taking calls amid other people especially when they are within earshot. Move to a private quiet place away from the crowd, remember no one wants to hear your conversation. Where this is impractical, the other option is to speak softly.
- Avoid making calls calling too early and too late. What is too early or too late is subjective. However, between 08:00 AM and 06:00 PM may be reasonable and will depend on the relationship between the two people. Etiquette dictates respect for other people's space and privacy. Making business calls that are not urgent at ungodly hours may be offensive and may put the integrity and finesse of the caller in question.

Letters and E-mail

E-mails

Correspondence is a conversation or communication in writing. Its content and tone will depend on factors like subject matter and relationship between the parties. Letters and emails must be clear, correctly constructed (with words in full) and properly punctuated. inundated with acronyms.

Like all communication, both social and business correspondence should clearly communicate the intended message, accompanied by an appropriate tone and words to keep the reader engaged. Even when a strong message must be communicated, necessary boundaries must be observed. The choice of words is critical. 'I hate you' has a stronger intonation than 'I don't like you'.

Avoid gossip, bad-mouthing, divulging confidential and private information about others as well as obscene and outrightly offensive language in any manner of correspondence. Always remember that anything in writing may be seen by eyes beyond the intended audience. The internet and other platforms like conventional correspondence (such as letters) are not fool proof and can end up in the wrong hands. Anything in writing is a permanent record and can be used against you, with potentially dire consequences.

Social media

Technology has shrunk distances. Everyone and everything are but a click away. Even video calls through various mediums can be made in real-time. Social media is a broad platform, open to the whole world, to people known and unknown, seen and unseen, making it difficult to regulate. Most of the available privacy options are not even foolproof.

A substantial part of social media platforms requires users to write, speak in real-time using voice notes, pictures, all of which are traceable to the author or initiator. Social media, because of its nature can be prone to abuse.

Social media has no tone. Unlike one-on-one

conversations where verbal and non-verbal cues are used during conversations, which enable people to understand each other, social media does not enjoy that privilege, making the user prone to being misunderstood. It becomes important to exercise caution in the content including the choice of words used online.

Social media and the content that is posted on it is permanent and once the 'send' button is clicked, it is gone and it's too late. It can't be retracted. The careless and irresponsible use of social media has the potential to cause irreparable damage, hence the need to observe proper rules of etiquette in such fora.

It is not unusual for people to post personal information and pictures of themselves and their families on the internet. Some depict lavish lifestyles, happy marriages and families for all to see. Publications on the internet are in effect publications to the whole world. Heinous crimes have been committed, fuelled by content posted on social media, lives have been lost and families shattered over content innocently and intentionally posted on the internet without thinking or anticipating the consequences of doing so. Even soaring businesses have plummeted over careless social media publications and the use of social media. Caution should therefore be exercised in publishing too much personal information.

Etiquette dictates that personal information published on the internet must be posted on a need-to-know basis and not just for anyone out there. The internet has made conducting due diligence on individuals so much easier. The content that you post on social media speaks volumes about you. Remember there is no opportunity to defend yourself from the impression you create of yourself on social media.

There is another category of people who are in the habit of making inconsiderate remarks about other people and issues even when it's clearly none of their business and in total disregard for the feelings of others. Scathing attacks on the character and reputation of defenceless people are not appropriate. Words once spoken or written cannot be taken back. Fair comment on what is necessary and constructive is what is the acceptable norm.

Etiquette dictates the fair, responsible and constructive use of social media bearing in mind the potential ramifications of its abuse.

CHAPTER 6
MEETINGS

The meetings can be a lot of fun, or they can be
frustrating' — Bod Weir

Generally, meetings are categorized as social, formal or
informal. The nature, agenda and venue will determine
the dress code and general conduct of the meeting.

Seating

The rule of thumb in any event involving seating,
whether office, home or otherwise is to wait for the
host to seat you. Or at least, ask if and where you may
be seated. When there are several guests and you have
not been ushered or offered a seat, it is good etiquette
to ask about the seating arrangement, that is whether
it's free seating or not.

Timekeeping

One of life's Platinum Rules is timekeeping. The habit of timekeeping is invaluable. It not only shows respect for the other person but is also symbolic of one's self-discipline. There's no act as despicable and as disrespectful as showing up late and expecting other people to adjust their time to suit yours. Other people's time is not your time. In the words of William Shakespeare, from his book, The Merry Wives of Windsor, 'better three hours too soon than a minute too late'. Time waits for one. Let's not waste our own, let alone that of others.

If you run late due to circumstances beyond your control, etiquette dictates that you phone ahead of the meeting and apologize. In the ordinary course of things, there should be no excuse for late coming.

Conduct of meetings

The conduct of meetings varies and will depend entirely on the nature of the meeting. Ordinarily, in formal setups, there is a facilitator who oversees and manages the agenda. The facilitator will open the meeting and introduce the persons present when they are meeting for the first time and thereafter highlight the essence of the meeting. Where there are protocols involved, the facilitator may open and delegate the management and conduct of the meeting to another person.

In an ideal set-up, people should be free to express themselves and air their views, save where there are protocols and other regulations for the conduct of meetings and where freedom of expression is curtailed. Etiquette dictates that, you do not have to say anything if you have nothing to contribute to the matter under discussion. It is only critical, well-meaning, and value-adding content that must be spoken.

Length of meetings

Longer meetings consume time and oft be exhausting. The greatest risk in holding long meetings is the loss of focus and attention. It is said that people's focus and attention shift with time. From 0-15 minutes, the focus span is said to be 91%, 15-30 minutes at 84% and 45 minutes and above reducing to 64%[iii] hence the need for an alert and diplomatic facilitator to curtail the time.

While there are generally no standard rules for conduct of meetings, there are certain generally accepted rules that must be adhered to. Generally, the rules applicable under Chapter 2 on conversations apply to meetings as well.

In a nutshell, be respectful of other people's views, beliefs, opinions and privacy. Allow others to freely air their views and listen attentively, responding only when you are permitted to do so.

There are still rules of etiquette that should be practiced no matter the circumstances or the degree of familiarity with the attendees.

Informal and social gatherings

Going out to meet with friends should be to refresh and catch up. The choice of company will always determine the quality of time spent at the social gathering.

People of all age groups, especially the young and middle-aged, will usually have a favourite spot at their local bar or at least other regular hang-out spots where they are probably known and have formed relationships with other regulars.

Paying for drinks

Women and men endure the same challenges and stresses of life. It is not unusual for a woman to take time off to unwind after a long hard day's work, using her own money, alone or with friends. When men folk have a level of interest in a lady at a social gathering, it is courteous to offer a drink, normally done to get her attention. Sometimes, the drink comes with an offer to join the table. Some women may find such an offer intrusive or outrightly offensive. It is necessary to exercise caution and assess the situation before proceeding with the offer. Rejection is painful. It is courteous to either directly or through any available staff at the facility, approach the person of interest and ask if they mind having a drink bought for them or to join them at their table.

On the other hand, for a woman to ask a stranger at a bar to buy a drink for her may be viewed as desperate and uncouth. Society is however evolving slowly in accepting equality between the genders, which may include the right of a woman to approach a man in some settings.

In a group, generally who pays the bill is dependent on the prevailing culture and in some cases status, perceived or otherwise, of the people present. In some instances, each guest present pays their own bill, in others, the host should offer to pay the bill.

There is a habit, especially among the younger female folk, where rather than show up at a date alone, they opt to carry along their friends, without informing their date and expecting him to foot their bills. This is unacceptable and may quite guarantee no future dates.

If you are uncomfortable going on a date alone, it is good manners to either let your date know you are tugging a friend along and to ask if he is fine with it. If he is not, go alone or rather stay home. There is nothing as ill-bred as imposing not only company but also unplanned expenditure on another.

Group meals and drinks

Payment for meals and drinks in group gatherings will depend on the circumstances and the relationship between the group members. In some, it is expected that the host will pay the bill while in others, each person pays for what they consume. It is only fair that there is clarity on who will pay for what prior to the gathering.

If you are not the one paying the bill, etiquette dictates exercising reasonableness and modesty in your choice of food and drink in so far as it relates to price, unless you are undoubtedly certain that the payer has deep pockets. This doesn't necessarily mean going for the cheapest meal.

The basic rule of thumb is always to carry enough money for your own food, drinks and where ensure that you have your transport arrangements solidly in place for your return home.

Bars and Pubs

Bars and pubs are more social places and conversations with strangers are rife. A customer that accepts a drink from a stranger is expected to chat with him at least until the drink is finished. It is always good etiquette to ask if it is alright to join another whether they are known to you or not.

Most of those that stand at bars are more open-bodied than those who are seated. It is good etiquette to offer a round of drinks where people around a table are taking turns to buy a round. Where for some reason one is unable to buy, they can ask to be left out for the time being. It is uncouth to just walk out without buying a round after you have consumed drinks bought by others, even if you are not an alcohol drinker. Never ever force another to drink when they don't want to and never force another to drink more than they want to drink.

While the increased consumption of alcohol can impair proper judgment, it is good etiquette to observe one's own alcohol intake as you drink and know when it's time to go home. Being overly intoxicated, especially in public may impact how you are perceived by others. There is nothing worse than waking up the next morning feeling guilty and wondering the extent of the damage you might have inflicted on your own reputation the previous evening because of excessive alcohol consumption.

It is prudent, when intending to drink in excess, to do it in the privacy of your home or that of other close friends or family, rather than in public. It is necessary to protect one's reputation. With the onset of phones and their videos, caution must be had in one's public conduct, lest you are unknowingly recorded dancing inappropriately or conducting yourself in some other societally 'unacceptable manner', running the risk of a leaked video which depending of your standing may be prejudicial. In Junius' words, 'the integrity of men is to be measured by their conduct, not by their professions.'

[iii] www.meetingking.com

CHAPTER 7
DINING

'The Goops they lick their fingers, and the Goops they lick their knives, they spill their broth on the tablecloth-Oh they lead disgusting lives!
The Goops they talk while eating, and loud and fast they chew, and that is why I'm glad that I am not Goop-Are you?' — Unknown

Dining and sharing meals have always been an integral part of every culture. Just as societies have evolved through technology, migration and other means, so have the traditional fundamentals of dining and cuisine.

Hosting

The conversation is the music of every sumptuous meal. The host must meet the guests and seat them. Good conversation triggers good energy and innately adds flavour to the meal. This is the reason why guests must be chosen cautiously when hosting like considering inviting guests that have things in common.

Décor' while appealing to the eye, may interfere with the conversation if it's too large and obstructive. Choose elegant centrepieces that are reasonably sized. Audible speech and eye contact during a conversation even at mealtime enhance good communication. Engaging in lively conversation at mealtimes enriches the dining experience.

As a host, your role is to make your guests feel comfortable. Hosting, therefore, calls for multi-tasking, patience and good cheer, as each guest will require a level of attention.

Placing of food

In the modern and contemporary setting such as a home or an ordinary restaurant, food is placed to the left of the dinner plate while glasses and as such drinks are placed to the right. Likewise, forks are also placed on the left side of the place and knives and spoons on the right.

Each course ordinarily has its own utensils or cutlery, in the book on The Essentials of Business Etiquette, Pachter writes, '*The largest fork is generally the entrée (starter) fork. The salad fork is smaller. The largest spoon is usually the soup spoon. If you are having a fish course, you may see the fish knife and fork as part of the place setting. The utensils above the plate are the dessert fork and spoon, although these may sometimes be placed on either side of the plate or brought in with the dessert.*"

Regardless of the circumstances, there are certain

common fundamental principles of dining etiquette:

DO NOT:

- Seat yourself, if being hosted, regardless, wait to be seated or ask for the seating arrangement.
- Eat before others, at a shared table it is prudent for everyone to begin eating at the same time, no matter how hungry one is, normally, the host should begin or motion to the table to start having the meal.
- Order messy or sticky foods like spareribs or other finger foods but rather opt for food requiring the use of fork and knife it is as they are neater, especially in formal dining set-ups.
- Pass the food randomly but rather pass the food to the right and not the left side of the table and use the words please and thank you.
- Eat while standing.
- Taste the food before you add salt or pepper.
- Cut all your food such as meat at once, but cut it bit by bit as you eat.
- Place used cutlery on the table but rest it on the plate.
- Chew with your mouth open.
- Place your elbows on the table. When not eating keep hands on laps and wrists on the edge of the table.
- Sit too far from the table.
- Force others to eat more than they want. It is acceptable to make a recommendation.
- Put bones on the table while eating but instead place them on the side of the plate or better still

ask for a side plate and never spit on your napkin or serviette.

- Put a knife in your mouth when eating.
- Bend under the table to pick food or cutlery that drops on the floor. Just let it be there and politely ask for alternative cutlery if its food just pick some more.
- Announce to others where you find a startling, misplaced object in the food such as an insect or hair strand, rather quietly motion to the person waiting at the table if in a restaurant or the host and ask for an alternative plate.
- Giggle or suppress laughter as it gives the impression of mocking those around you and shows insincerity. Similarly, loud uncontrolled laughter must always be avoided, unless it's a joke made for everyone's benefit.
- Leave the table while others are still eating, if you must, politely excuse yourself.
- Leave the ringtone on your phone on. As an option, activate the discreet function or reduce the volume.
- Eat at a moderate and not super speed.
- Slurp soup or juice or blow on a hot beverage or food. For soup gently scoop it from the bowl and sip it from the side of the spoon if it's too hot.
- Order excessive alcohol except for reasonable and acceptable quantities of wine that ordinarily accompany a meal.
- Smoke during meals.
- Cough out loud while eating, it is prudent to cover your mouth with your hand or serviette while turning your head away from the table and the

people next to you. It is advisable to decline an invitation to a meal or public gathering of any nature when you are suffering from a cold, there's nothing as imprudent as coughing and sneezing at the table and especially after the onset of Covid-19.

- Do not stack the plates when you are done with your meal, the host or the waiter must take up that responsibility, unless it is in an informal set-up.
- Compliment the host if you like the food but shut it if you don't.

For conversation during dining, refer to Chapter 2.

CHAPTER 8
VISITING

'Go often to the house of thy friend, for weeds choke the unused path'— Ralph Waldo Emerson

The hostess

There is nothing as uncouth as visiting someone's home or even work place, unannounced. Etiquette dictates that permission to visit must be sought from the host prior to any visit. This allows the host to prepare for the visitor well in advance. Regardless of the emotional attachment one has to any visitors, their presence requires adjustment of one's normal schedule. If you are in the habit of going to bed at 8 O'clock, you may have to adjust that time to entertain the visitor. When a request is made to be visited, if you as host is unprepared for the visitor, politely decline with a reason.

It is the host's duty to ensure that visitors feel warm

and comfortable. In a home, where the guest is not familiar with the environment, it is prudent to show them around the house or at least the essential areas such as the bathroom. Where the visitors are spending the night, then a more elaborate orientation should be done. The hostess should explain to the visitor the basic expected norms or lifestyle of the household and general practices like breakfast time and general options available to them. This however also depends on the relationship between the visitor and the visited and the purpose of the visit.

The guest

The guest must make sure that their intended length of stay is clearly communicated to their host and ensure that they stick to it unless otherwise beyond their control. From the outset, the visitor must know that visiting someone else entails adapting and accepting the hosts way of life and their values, including that of their children and household and must conduct themselves with courtesy and warmth. The temperamental visitor must leave his bad habits at the door as he enters another's home. The visitor who hates cats must not abuse the cute little kitten he finds resident in the home but must live around it. There is nothing as annoying as a visitor who attempts to make another person's home an extension of their own.

Where necessary, the visitor should offer to help with some chores such as cooking and cleaning or at least anything that might be required. When it comes to cooking, it is important to confirm how the host prefers their meals prepared even if it means the manner of cutting vegetables. Don't assume that your cooking is the best. Unless you are outrightly asked to prepare a meal. When in doubt, ask. Homes are sacred places. Observe boundaries and respect the host's privacy.

The visitor must clean their bath and make their own bed in the morning. During their stay, especially if it is for a couple of days or longer, they can even offer to buy groceries or render any other help if they have the means. The guest must avoid being an absolute liability to the host. These rules are not cast in concrete but depend on the relationship between the host and guest and the prevailing circumstances. A visitor must not make the visiting experience a pain or nuisance for the host. Entertaining people can be a lot of work.

When leaving the host's home, the good guest must thank the host for hosting them and give them space before the next visit.

Visits to the hospital

Hospitals the world over have prescribed visiting hours. Patients need time to rest and recoup from their illnesses. The support of family and friends is critical during such times. Time spent visiting the sick depends on the relationship the visitor has with the patient. Long visits may exhaust the patient and be detrimental to their recovery. Make the visit short and meaningful.

What to take

It is always safer to take neutral gifts like flowers, fruits or a humorous book, subject to the patient's condition and hospital regulations.

Avoid carrying cooked food as this is ordinarily a preserve for close family and friends. A friend living close to the hospital took it upon herself to make soup for a sick brother-in-law who had been admitted for a couple of days. A few hours later she called the patient's wife to check up on him. Her response, 'he was doing fine until he ate the soup you brought'. Fortunately, he survived 'the soup' and in fact recovered, dying months later from other causes and not the soup. With that experience was followed by a vow never to prepare a meal for any sick person regardless of how close, ever again.

Conversation

It is not in a regular visitor's place to pry into details of the patient's condition unless the patient volunteer's this information.

Hospital conversation should be uplifting. Energy is transferable. People can feel bad energy this includes fear, pity or other negative emotions. Shedding tears and speaking of the afterlife or death in full view or within the earshot of the patient is not appropriate. Visitors should keep their stay short and avoid engaging the sick person in endless conversation.

CHAPTER 9
DOMESTIC HELPERS

'When you treat waiters, maids and your subordinates with humbleness and respect, it actually elevates your status'— Ekra Khan

Helpers form a part of our lives and over time become family. Like everywhere, domestic helpers have diverse backgrounds. In this context, the term domestic help will refer to nannies, maids, butlers, housekeepers and gardeners, or any other helper deployed to assist in the management of the household.

Whatever the case any helper within the household should be treated with respect and in a considerate and humane manner. Even children must be taught to respect the house helpers, of course within reasonable boundaries. They are usually the first point of call even in emergencies.

From the date of recruitment, their Terms of

Engagement should be clearly communicated, including the do's and don'ts.

Helpers can sometimes cause untold stress and misery to their employers as well. While it is important to show them kindness and empathy, clear boundaries must be drawn. Avoid over-familiarity. The expected dress code and conduct must be clearly defined. Appropriate clothing for house helpers must be always worn. A home must always be orderly. Never cease to supervise, through inadequate supervision, loopholes for compromised work quality and sometimes culminating in the creation of parallel structures within the home. Never put temptation in the helper's way. Caution must be had in the safe keeping of money within the house.

Roles and clear boundaries between the helpers and the children and their parents must also be drawn. History is filled with stories of romances that have blossomed between employer and helpers some of which have devastated families.

The domestic helpers must also ensure that they comply with the rules of the household and respect the members of the household, including their children, visitors and animals, while maintaining the necessary boundaries.

CHAPTER 10
PUBLIC ETIQUETTE

'Freedom without rules doesn't work. And communities do not work unless they are regulated by etiquette.' — Judith Martin

Queuing

The rule is that the last person arriving must stand at the back of the queue. It is ill-mannered and outrightly disrespectful to even attempt to cut in a queue. The same applies to traffic jams. If anyone cuts in the queue, you are within your rights to politely advise them to stand behind the queue. If for any reason you must cut the line, there is no harm in politely asking the person(s) in front, if you can go before them giving a reason for your request, such as you are about to miss your flight.

Walking

The safest and most reasonable place for pedestrians to walk is on the pavement or sidewalk.

It is important to always observe safety rules. The rule of thumb is that you walk facing the traffic as you can observe oncoming traffic. When it is dark wear bright colours such as white or an outfit with a reflector to provide clear visual and for your safety. Be respectful of other road users, including pedestrians, runners and cyclists. Avoid using earphones while walking as they can be distracting and hazardous. Pay attention to your environment and avoid the phone.

If you're walking with a dog, keep it on a short leash. Do not let it interfere with the peaceful enjoyment of other road users. For your own safety avoid secluded areas and rather use those well-travelled. Be aware of people around and give way where you must.

Dancing

Lyall Watson says, dancing is surely the most basic and relevant of all forms of expression. Nothing else can so effectively give outward form to an inner experience.

To dance is innate in humans. This is evident from little children, who before they comprehend music, are instinctively able to move their little bodies at the sound of music. We are all born with a dance. Dance comes in a variety of styles. In Africa, traditional celebrations were always characterized by songs and reverberating drums. Dance like music bears no judgment, does not discriminate but brings people together in its appreciation.

While we can play the loudest music and dance the

wildest dances in the privacy of our homes, like several other things, we must question when it is appropriate to dance in public. One's conduct in public, irrespective of the beat or tempo, is often a test of one's refinement.

Dance especially in public must always be kept modest. There is no rule of thumb. Sometimes, circumstances will allow for one's full expression in dance. It all depends on the circumstances. Certain dances require a particular skill set, don't agree to participate if you don't comprehend the rules. The Angolan people of Southwest Africa have a dance popularly called Kizomba which is an intimate dance, executed between man and woman, requiring a special skill that no untrained person should publicly dare.

In the words of William Purkey, 'you've gotta dance like there's nobody watching.' While we must flex those muscles, boundaries must be drawn even in the dancing. Formal events dictate more formal and toned-down dancing. Informal events are more open, and the environment will determine how expressive and energetic your dance can be.

The rule of thumb is that modest dance moves are permissible in public. However, the more erotic dances should be reserved for more intimate spaces.

Other forms of inappropriate public conduct

Privacy is every human being's entitlement. In public, certain rules of conduct must be adhered to. Avoiding habits that disturb other people's peace such as singing, arguing, speaking loudly, bragging, use of obscene and offensive language, speaking on the phone while having a conversation with others, playing loud music, videos and unreasonable honking. The rule is, when in public, give the people around some peace and quiet and respect their privacy.

CHAPTER 11
DEATHS AND FUNERALS

Death

Death is inevitable. As goes the saying, there are two certain things in life — death and taxes.

After Death

The death of a person is normally followed by informal notifications like the phone or word of mouth among close relatives and friends. Others may opt to place Death Notices in the print media. Very close relatives and friends must be informed of the death in person and not through the phone or a third party as these aids in managing the trauma that such devastating news may have on an individual.

Registration of Death

It is normally a requirement that deaths, like births, should be registered by the Registrar or its equivalent usually in the district in which the death occurs and after ascertaining the cause of death and certificate is issued by a doctor. Where the cause of death is in doubt such as sudden, unnatural or violent deaths these are reported to the coroner who must ascertain the cause of death before a certificate is issued and burial can take place.

Mourning

Again, the manner of mourning differs from culture to culture. In some parts of Africa for example, the women will normally wear wrappers and head scarves as they attend the funeral house. Where appropriate sombre colours such as purple and black and modest dress must be worn at funerals. This includes jewellery and fragrances must be modest.

Donations

Funerals are sometimes sudden, unexpected and inevitably require a level of expenditure, especially if not covered by an insurance or other funeral plan. It is courteous to offer help to the family in one form or another during the funeral.

Burial

The norm is to bury loved ones at a designated cemetery. The determination of alternative ways of disposing of bodies such as cremation is dependent on factors like religion and the personal wishes of the deceased person. Burials are usually attended by close friends and family and in some cases, upon invitation. During the burial, it is important to show respect for the dead in dress, manner and speech. Speaking and laughing loudly, lurid ring tones, inappropriate dress and uncontrolled wailing should be avoided.

And when all is said and done, if there's an art to be learnt which carries no risks, but only an abundance of benefits, it is etiquette. Learn it!

REFERENCES

Allen, Betty, If you please! A book of Manners for Young Moderns, Philadelphia, J.B. Lippincott Company, 1942.

Barnes, James, Etiquette for the well-dressed man, Sussex, Copper Beech Publishing, 31 October 2001.

Buehner, Caralyn, It's a Spoon, not a Shovel; Dial Books, New York, 1995.

Clark, Mary, Etiquette, Garden City, New York, 1857

Eyebright, Daisy, A Manual of Etiquette with Hints of Politeness and Good Breeding, Dodo Press, 1874.

Hartley, Florence, The Ladies' Book of Etiquette and Manual of Politeness: A complete handbook for the use of the lady in polite society, E-Book; #35123, January 30 2011

Pachter, Barbara, The Essentials of Business Etiquette, New York, McGraw Hill, July 30 2013.

Post, Lizzy et al, Emily Post's Manners for Today, 19th edition, New York, William Morrow, 25th April 2017.

Roosevelt, Eleanor, Book of Common sense Etiquette, New York, Macmillan, 1962

ABOUT THE AUTHOR

Charlotte Mweemba, an ardent reader, is a Zambian-based lawyer having worked in both public and private sectors. Charlotte has always been passionate about writing, and *Etiquette Gems Revealed* is her first book publication. She holds a bachelor of law degree and a master's in business administration.

Printed in Great Britain
by Amazon